Estonia

Russian
Federation

Mazsalaca

Gauja

Latvia

Daugava

Aiviekste

Daugava

Belarus

656 ft
1640 ft
- 3281 ft
- 4921 ft

Daugavpils

Looking at Europe

Latvia

Amanda Aizpuriete

The Oliver Press, Inc.
Minneapolis

This edition published in 2006 by The Oliver Press, Inc.
Charlotte Square
5707 West 36th Street
Minneapols, MN 55416-2510
USA

Published by arrangement with KIT Publishers, The Netherlands, and
The Evans Publishing Group, London, UK, 2005

Library of Congress Cataloging-in-Publication Data

Aizpuriete, Amanda.
    Latvia / Amanda Aizpuriete.
        p. cm. -- (Looking at Europe)
    Includes index.
    Contents: History -- The country -- Towns and cities -- People and culture -- Education
    -- Cuisine -- Transportation -- The economy -- Nature -- Latvia in Europe.
    ISBN 1-881508-37-4
    1. Latvia--Juvenile literature. I. Title. II. Series.

DK504.23.A37 2006
947.96--dc22

                                                        2006040087

Text: Amanda Aizpuriete
Photographs: Jan Willem Bultje
Translation: Katarina Hartgers
US editing: Holly Day
Design and Layout: Grafisch Ontwerpbureau Agaatsz BNO, Meppel, The Netherlands
Cover: Icon Productions, Minneapolis, USA
Cartography: Armand Haye, Amsterdam, The Netherlands
Production: J & P Far East Productions, Soest, The Netherlands

Picture Credits
All images courtesy of KIT Publishers except:
p. 9(b) © Anna Clopet/CORBIS; p. 14 © Niall Benvie/CORBIS; p. 28 © Peter
Turnley/CORBIS; p. 35(b) © Steve Raymer/CORBIS; p. 46 © Staffan Widstrand/
CORBIS; p. 47(t) © Petr Josek/Reuters/CORBIS; p.45 (t) Oskars Petersons; p.47: NATO

ISBN 1-881508-37-4
Printed in Singapore
10 09 08 07 06   8 7 6 5 4 3 2 1

Contents

Introduction

Latvia – officially called the Republic of Latvia – is a country in north-central Europe. It is a mainly flat land, with a few hills and no mountains. Small villages with traditional houses are scattered across the countryside, but the big cities are thriving industrial and tourist centers.

Latvia is one of the three Baltic states lying on the coast of the Baltic Sea. The others are Lithuania and Estonia. Latvia is bordered in the north by Estonia, in the south by Lithuania, in the east and south-east by Russia and Belarus, and in the west by the Baltic Sea.

This area has been inhabited since the Stone Age. Over the centuries, many different peoples have invaded, conquered and settled in the region that is now Latvia. The result of this can be seen in the cosmopolitan air of many of the towns and cities. In fact, in the capital, Riga, only one third of the population speaks Latvian as a first language, although in rural areas, Latvian is still spoken by most people. There is a strong Russian influence in the country. Russians settled here in the eighteenth century, and the country was under Soviet Russian rule for a large part of the twentieth century.

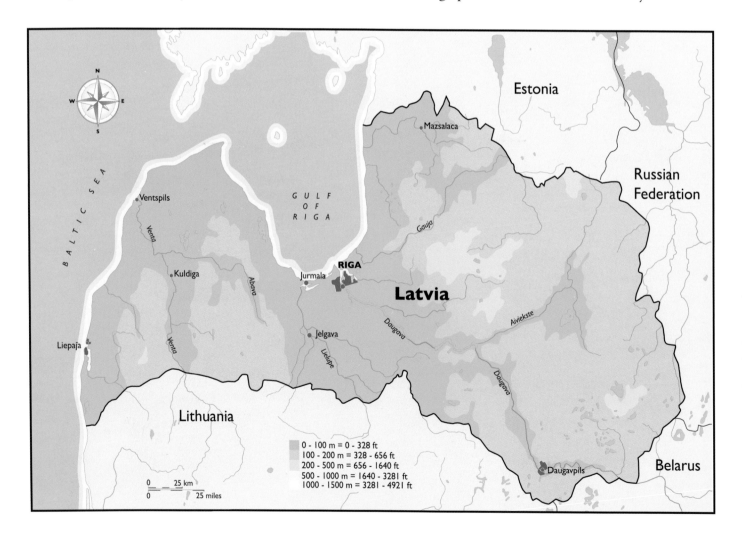

► *Conifer trees line the beaches of Latvia's Baltic coastline.*

Although it spent many years under foreign rule, Latvia gained independence in 1991. Today, several old customs are experiencing a revival, and this can be seen in the many festivals held throughout the year, in which people wear traditional dress and feast on traditional dishes.

Despite this, Latvia is a forward-thinking country and is welcoming the boom in technologies such as computers, the Internet, and mobile phones. Industry is thriving and the economy is improving.

Latvia was accepted as a full member of the European Union (EU) in 2004. This has helped to open up new opportunities for trade and international relations, particularly with other members of the EU.

▼ *Latvia has been an important trade route between other countries for centuries, and still is today.*

History

The land that is now the country of Latvia was inhabited as early as the Stone Age. The tribes from which the Latvian people are descended came to the area around 2300 BC. These people had basic agricultural skills, and hunted animals in the large forests and fished in the rivers and lakes.

▼ *Almost every town in Latvia has a museum exhibiting ancient finds, such as these old stone tools.*

Until the Middle Ages, settlers in Latvian territory lived in a handful of separate provinces. The three main tribes were the Latgals, the Zemgals and the Courlanders. There was some trade between these tribes, and the Courlanders also had trading agreements with the Scandinavian countries. However, these contacts did not stop them from raiding and robbing each other. A Scandinavian story called *Egil's Saga*, believed to have been written in the thirteenth century, tells the story of the Viking Egil's voyage to Courland. It describes how he was attacked and imprisoned by the natives and made a daring escape.

German rule

In the thirteenth century, an order of knights from Germany called the Livonian Brothers of the Sword invaded Latvia, with the intention of converting the people to Christianity. The Latvian tribes fought hard to repel the invaders. Battles took place and many lives were lost, but the knights promised the pagan Latvians that their sins would be forgiven if they surrendered, and they had soon conquered much of the territory. Today, only ruins remain of the stone churches and castles that were built by the conquerors in the late thirteenth century. Several chronicles were written at the time in honor of the Latvian tribal chieftains and the battles they won against the Germans.

▶ *These ancient coins come from the Livonia region, established by the German knights. Livonia covered parts of present-day Latvia and Estonia.*

Livonijas ordenis

It was not long before many German merchants and tradesmen flooded to the region, realizing that its location on the Baltic coast offered good trading opportunities. Many Latvian cities flourished during German rule, and trade developed with countries in both Europe and the east. However, German rule also had its drawbacks. In the city of Riga, now the capital of Latvia, only Germans were appointed to high offices, although later on Latvians were also granted the right to practice certain trades. Others, however, were reduced to the status of slaves.

Swedish rule

In the seventeenth century, Swedes and Poles invaded and settled in Latvia. The period of Swedish rule saw a change in fortunes for many Latvians. Farmers' children were allowed to attend school, and books – including the Bible – were printed for the first time in the Latvian language. The province of Courland in particular flourished. Explorers from this area sailed to the coasts of Africa and America. They set up trading and storage facilities in Gambia, on the west coast of Africa. Another Courland colony was established on Tobago in the West Indies, and many Courlanders worked on the plantations there. Some words in the language spoken on Tobago still sound Latvian, and the arrival of the Latvian colonists is re-enacted every year at a local festival.

▼ The city of Riga was once ruled by the German aristocracy. Today it is the capital of Latvia.

▲ Castle Mālbork in Poland was the headquarters of the Livonian Brothers of the Sword. Their mission was to convert the inhabitants of the Baltic regions to Christianity.

In 1700, the Great Northern War broke out. The Russian army, under Tsar Peter the Great, invaded Latvia and conquered the city of Riga. Within 20 years, large parts of Latvia had been completely destroyed. At the same time, an outbreak of the plague killed many inhabitants, leaving some regions almost uninhabited. As a result of the war, the region of Vidzeme and Riga became part of the Russian Empire.

The battle for independence

The Germans had remained a powerful presence and in the same century, German writers and philosophers began to criticize the way the Germans treated the Latvian people. The situation was slowly changing, though, and by the nineteenth century, Latvians were permitted to study at the University of Terbatas in Estonia. This was also the time when the first Latvian writers and poets became known. They refused to simply rewrite German literature and poetry, and instead produced works about their own country in their own language.

▲ *The unveiling of the monument to Tsar Peter the Great in 1910, attended by Tsar Nicolas II.*

They were supported to a certain extent by the Russian tsar, who wished to abolish serfdom in his territories. But the tsar was obstructed by the Russian nobility, who did not want the Latvians to regain the land Russia now held. They devised a plan which meant that even when the Latvian farmers were granted freedom, they would still have no rights to land or a house.

In 1905, a revolution broke out among the Latvian people, who were frustrated by continuing Russian rule in their country. Workers went on strike and peasants burned down many manor houses then owned by the Russians and Germans. The authorities reacted harshly and many Latvians were sent into exile in Siberia.

There were more hard times ahead for the Latvian people. During the First World War (1914–18), more than half the population fled the country as German troops invaded Latvian lands.

◀ *The Freedom Monument, or Statue of Liberty, in Riga commemorates the fight for Latvian independence.*

The road to democracy

By the end of the First World War, the Russian Empire had collapsed, and this offered a great opportunity for the Latvian people to push for their country's independence. All three Baltic states – Latvia, Lithuania and Estonia – announced their independence in 1918. By 1920, all foreign armies had been withdrawn from Latvian territory, and the Russians had recognized Latvia's independence. The Latvian constitution was accepted, and the first president was chosen. Over the next 20 years science, the arts and culture flourished in Latvia.

The Second World War broke out in 1939, and in 1940, Russian troops once again invaded Latvia. Within a short time, Latvia became a province of the USSR. Latvian territories were also occupied by German troops between 1941 and 1944, but this time many Latvians saw the Germans as their allies, fighting against Soviet Russia. However, at the end of the war, the USSR was on the winning side, and was granted Latvia as part of the post-war settlement.

Apart from a few years in between the world wars, Latvian territory had been occupied by one ruling force after another. There was little improvement under the new Soviet regime. At first some lands were returned to the peasants, but soon the Russians insisted that farmland become state property. People were forced to work together on collective farms owned by the communist regime. All other resources and industries were nationalized under Soviet rule.

▲ Latvian men volunteer as soldiers to fight the invading Germans during the First World War.

▲ During the Second World War, many Latvians saw the German invaders as liberators of their country.

However, the Latvian people had tasted independence, and after so many years of war and foreign rule, they wanted their country back. Once again, the three Baltic states began working towards regaining independence. In 1990, the people of Latvia rejected their status as part of the USSR, and re-established the constitution that had been put in place in 1922.

The country finally achieved independence the following year. A new parliament, president, and prime minister were elected, and Latvia became a member of the United Nations. In 2004, the country was accepted as a member of both NATO and the European Union.

◀ Latvians hold up banners demanding independence for their country in the 1980s.

The country

Latvia (Republika Latvija) is a small country of only 24,938 square miles. It is 130 miles wide and 280 miles long. Latvia has approximately 2.3 million inhabitants, and a population density of about 96 people per square mile. Its closest neighbors are the other two Baltic states – Estonia to the north and Lithuania to the south.

Latvia, Lithuania, and Estonia were once inhabited by a tribe called the Balts, and Latvians and Lithuanians are descendants of this tribe. In Latvian, the word *balts* means "white," but in Latvian folksongs the word is often used to mean "good" or "dear." The Baltic Sea may have gained its name because of the white ice that covers it in the winter.

▶ *Latgale is a region in the east of Latvia, lying to the north of the Daugava River.*

▼ *A farming village in the northeast of Latvia. The fields have been harvested as winter approaches.*

◀ *The Daugava River, near Daugavpils, in the southeast of the country*

The names of the original Latvian tribes can still be found on a map of Latvia. Latvia has four provinces. The rural Kurzeme lies in the west, where the Kursi tribe used to live. Latgale is in the east, and is named after the Latgals. This area contains many rivers and lakes. The fertile plains are located in the Zemgale province, where the castles of the rulers of Zemgale used to be. The fourth province, in the north, is Vidzeme – a very hilly area. Vidzeme means "the middle of the country." The capital, Riga, is located in this province.

Landscape

The Latvian landscape is largely flat, with a few rolling hills. About 40 percent of the country is covered with forests. These are varied, with dark pine trees interspersed with large oaks, birches, and aspen trees. The forests are some of Latvia's greatest natural attractions and are particularly beautiful in the autumn when the leaves turn red and gold. The forests alternate with pasture and agricultural areas. Latvia is also a land of water, and there are many lakes and rivers. The coastline is unspoiled and has many fine beaches.

Latvia does not have any high mountains, but it has a few notable hills. The highest of these is Gaizinkalns (1,023 feet), which is located in Vidzeme. This hill is very popular with skiers and tourists, and many Latvians refer to Gaizinkalns as a mountain rather than a hill. This area is often called the Vidzeme Switzerland because of the similarity between the beautiful landscapes here and those in Switzerland.

▶ *Jaunpils Castle lies in the Tukums region, which is located on the boundary between the Vidzeme and Kurzeme provinces. This is the only castle of the German Livonian Order that is still standing.*

◀ The Daugava River, also known as the Western Dvina

Rivers

Latvia contains many rivers and lakes. In fact, the Latgale area in the east of the country has been nicknamed the "blue river land" because of the abundance of water there.

The widest river in Latvia is the Daugava. In the past, many settlements grew up along its shores, and these are now towns and cities. The capital, Riga, lies on the banks of the Daugava and is the river's main port. The Daugava stretches for 635 miles. It rises in Russia and flows south and west through Belarus and Latvia, eventually reaching the Gulf of Riga, a branch of the Baltic Sea.

The *nāves sala* ("island of death") is also located on the Daugava, not far from Riga. This strip of land got its name during the First World War. The front line in this part of Europe ran along the Daugava, and Latvian riflemen fought against German soldiers here for two years. In the end, the Germans used poisonous gas to win the battle. This was the first place a modern chemical weapon was used.

Several hydroelectric power plants are found along the Daugava. The oldest was built in 1936. The Daugava often floods in spring, when the snow on the fields, in the forests, and along the river banks melts. But these floods are never catastrophic. It is fascinating to watch the large ice floes collide and disappear in the direction of the sea.

The fairy-tale Daugava

Many Latvian folk stories tell about the strong Lāčplēsis, who was born and raised on the shore of the Daugava. Lāčplēsis' mother was a bear, and he inherited her bear ears, which gave him extraordinary powers. Lāčplēsis performed many heroic tasks. He cleansed the shores of the Daugava of monsters and wizards. In his last fight, his opponent, a black knight, cut off one of his ears. Lāčplēsis and his opponent fell into the depths of the river. According to legend, the battle continues under the water. When Lāčplēsis finally defeats the black knight, the Latvian people will regain their freedom.

The Gauja River in northeastern Latvia is winding and treacherous, with sand banks, estuaries, and high sandstone rocks along its shores. Some of the most famous Latvian landscapes lie along this river as its course runs through the national park of the same name.

▶ The Gauja River

The largest river in the Kurzeme region is the Venta, which flows through the old capital of Kuldiga. In the middle of this area lies the most famous waterfall in Latvia – the "Ventas Rumba." There are no high dramatic waterfalls in Latvia, and the Ventas Rumba is really just a stairway of dolomites (mineral rocks), 328 feet wide and almost 7 feet high. Many inhabitants of Kuldiga swim near the waterfall in summer. It is possible to stand on the stones in the middle of it and feel the water of the Venta River rushing down the stairway.

Latvia's most peaceful river is the Lielupe, which flows through the Zemgale plain. The Lielupe begins at the town of Bauska, where the Musa and Memele rivers meet. It eventually joins the Gulf of Riga and the Daugava River. The Lielupe is bordered by fields of wheat and meadows where cows and goats graze. It was here that the Zemgal tribe once lived.

▲ *The name Lielupe means "big river." It stretches for 74 miles.*

▼ *The Ventas Rumba waterfall reaches 328 feet across the Venta River in the Kurzeme region.*

Lakes

There are more than 3,000 lakes in Latvia. Nearly half of them are located in the eastern part of the country.

Latvia's deepest lake, the Dridzis, lies in the Latgale region. It is almost 215 feet deep, but the waters are very clear. Close to the lake stands Sun Mountain (692 feet high). From the summit, there is a view of about 30 lakes lying between the hills of Latgale. The largest lake is Lubans, and the area around the lake is an important wetlands area – home to many species of birds. The Devil's Lake, also in Latgale, lies in the middle of a dark forest. The lake got its name because its waters seem to change color depending on the weather. The water looks green when it is sunny, and becomes black when the weather is bad.

The Usma Lake lies in Kurzeme. The lake is part of the oldest nature reserve in the country – Moricsala, which was established in 1912.

▼ *A traditional wooden house sits on the banks of a small lake near the town of Smiltene. Here, in the northeastern part of the country, there are hundreds of lakes like this.*

Climate

Latvia has a mild climate. Summers can be cool, although it is not unusual for it to grow hot in the midday sun. The average temperature in summer is 61°F, but it can rise to 86°F around noon. The lakes and rivers also warm up, as does the rather shallow Baltic Sea along the coastline. The swimming season usually begins in the second half of June and lasts until the end of August. Nights are short in the summer, and the sun takes a long time to go down.

Winters in Latvia are quite cold. In December, temperatures can drop to -11°F, although the average is around 23°F. Snow will stay on the ground for almost three months. There are many good ski slopes in hilly areas, but they often have to be sprayed with artificial snow – especially in autumn. Latvia experiences wet winters, with frequent rain showers. March signals the beginning of spring, when the first crocuses and snowdrops appear. Latvia has about 70 days of sunshine and 180 days of rain each year.

▲ *A bobsled track in Sigulda, known as the "Switzerland of Vidzeme"*

◀ *Pastureland with a stork's nest supported by poles. Storks are a common sight in rural areas in the spring, and although they normally make their nests on telephone poles, some people build special structures like this for them (see page 44).*

Towns and cities

Although many towns and cities in Latvia have suffered from the damage caused by invasion and war over the centuries, in recent years, some of them have been carefully restored. In many places, several old buildings have survived to tell the tale of the different peoples who have lived in them.

Riga

Riga is Latvia's capital and its largest city, with a population of around 800,000. Located on the Gulf of Riga, an inlet of the Baltic Sea, the city is a major port and a thriving industrial and cultural center. There has been a settlement here for centuries, since the Baltic tribes set up a trading post in the area in the early thirteenth century. The original city of Vecriga can still be found in the heart of Riga. The cobbled streets here are named after the tradesmen who worked and sold their wares centuries ago – barrelmakers, tailors, and smiths.

◀ *The largest church in Riga is the cathedral — its foundation stone was laid in 1211. It houses a famous organ, which has 6,718 pipes, and many concerts are held here.*

One of the many legends about Riga tells of a beautiful long-haired girl who walks through the streets of the city once every 100 years, asking everyone she meets: "Has Riga been completed yet?" If anyone ever answers that the city has been completed, it will immediately disappear into the ground.

Latvian tradition says that when a church tower is completed, the builder should sit on the top, drink a glass of wine and then throw the glass down. The number of shards created when the glass shatters determines the number of years that the tower will stand. When the builder did this from the tower of the Church of St. Peter, a wagon filled with hay passed the church and the glass fell into it, remaining whole. People were afraid this meant that the tower would only stand for one year. In fact, it stood for about 200 years. Both the church and tower burned down during the Second World War. Since then, they have been rebuilt.

◀ *The Church of St. Peter, which has been rebuilt several times since it was first constructed in the thirteenth century*

The city of Riga was first mentioned in documents dated August 18, 1201. Before that, an old Livonian village was located where Riga now lies, on the Ridzene River. As the city grew, the Ridzene River was filled in. Riga and its surroundings now make up a province in their own right, and around one third of the Latvian population lives in this area.

There are many churches in Riga, and their spires and towers dominate the skyline. One of the most famous is the Church of St. Peter. Construction on it began in the first half of the thirteenth century. The wooden tower was built in the fifteenth century, and was the highest tower in Europe at the time. It collapsed in 1666. A new tower was built which was almost as high, but this tower was destroyed after being struck by lightning. It was rebuilt again in 1746.

In the Second World War, all the buildings around the town hall square burned down. The 200-year-old Town Hall with its library of thousands of books and the beautiful Black Head House also went up in flames. The Association of Black Heads was founded in the thirteenth century by foreign merchants. The lavish balls that were organized there were attended by Riga's high society.

▶ *Riga is one of the most popular tourist destinations in Latvia.*

 Restaurants, cafés, and shops line the streets of Riga's old and new towns.

Riga's old town is certainly beautiful. Old walls, window adornments, towers of different heights and styles, museums and cafés can all be found along the Daugava River. Riga's new town, however, is much larger. Here, there is the magnificent opera building, which has recently been renovated. Theater plays an important part in the lives of the Latvians, and many people attend plays in the capital. They also like to shop in the pavilions in the central market place. The pavilions were originally built as hangars for German airships, and were left empty by the German army after the First World War. Today, many types of Latvian produce are sold in these gigantic halls, and it is often possible to taste some of the foods before buying.

▲ The Black Head House has been rebuilt since the Second World War, and now houses collections of works of art.

Liepāja

Liepāja lies to the southwest of Riga, on the Baltic coast. The city was founded by the German knights in 1263, and had grown to become an important naval port by the late nineteenth century. Liepāja was occupied by the Germans during the First World War and for most of the Second World War, and it suffered severe damage during these periods. However, several old buildings have survived, including a number of churches.

Around 1890, Tsar Alexander III ordered the construction of a strong fortress and a naval port just outside Liepāja. Around the fortress, houses and buildings were built to accommodate the families of the Russian navy officers. The city was named Karosta ("Naval Port") and became a place of great strategic importance.

◀ The sign welcoming people to Liepāja

▲ The Russian Orthodox church in the fortress just outside Liepāja

▲ Part of the garrison where Russian naval officers and their families lived in the nineteenth century

However, after the Russians left, the city became a ghost town, sheltering homeless people. Nowadays, Karosta is experiencing a revival. New people are coming in, houses are being renovated, and the beautiful Russian Orthodox church has been restored.

Many Latvian pop stars attended the music school in Liepāja, and music is an important feature of the city. During the Soviet occupation, the Liepāja Dzintars – a huge outdoor music festival – was held here. Nowadays, concerts by local and international groups are often organized in the open-air theater, Put Vejini.

▼ The naval port at Karista was built under the orders of the Russian tsar. Most recently, it has been occupied by NATO.

◀ The bus station in Daugavpils. This is a thriving industrial area, close to the border with Lithuania.

Daugavpils

Daugavpils is the second-largest city in Latvia (after Riga), with around 110,000 inhabitants. It lies in southeast Latvia, on the Daugava River. In the sixteenth century, Daugavpils was an important commercial center, right at the crossroads of various trade routes. Very few buildings from that period are still standing, but it remains an important industrial town and transport route through the country.

Mazsalaca

Mazsalaca is a small town in the Vidzeme region, located on the Salaca River in northern Latvia. The town is well known as part of the Skanais Kalns National Park, and as a place of many old customs and traditions. Along the river in this region there are wooden sculptures of fairytale characters, each one symbolizing a myth or legend about important places in Latvia. These include the supernatural creature Kurbads, who single-handedly battled against evil spirits and monsters. The museum of the famous local sculptor Valters Hirte is in Mazsalaca, and it contains more than 200 sculptures of wooden devils.

About two miles from Mazsalaca town center stands the Werewolf Pine. This tree has one large and one small hole in it. Legend says that whoever can crawl through each hole three times will receive incredible powers. However, anyone who crawls through these holes during a full moon will change into a werewolf.

Not far away is the "Stairway of Dreams," a popular place for lovers to meet. In the valley below there is a "love bridge." Tradition says that lovers must stand on the bridge and make a wish, then run down the Stairway of Dreams with their eyes closed, while counting the steps. Once they have reached the bottom, if they have counted the steps correctly and can remember their wish, it will come true. There is also the Devil's Cave here, in which there is a spring that is believed to have healing properties.

▶ The Stairway of Dreams near Mazsalaca is a popular place for lovers to make a wish together.

◀ *Jūrmala is home to the largest water theme park in northern Europe.*

Jūrmala

Jūrmala lies on the Baltic coastline and has grown up out of the handful of fishing villages that were once scattered around this area. It now takes up 22 miles of the coastline. Many people are moving out of Riga to Jūrmala because it lies only 12 miles from the capital, but offers more opportunities for relaxation and fun.

Jūrmala is actually made up of a string of resorts, all of which are popular tourist destinations, with many hotels, cafés, and restaurants. The sandy beaches, facing the Gulf of Riga, are some of the main attractions along this stretch. The swimming season lasts for the whole year here, although the water can get cold sometimes when a southern wind blows the warm water away from the coast. Two of Jūrmala's beaches fly the blue flag that indicates that they comply with international standards. These beaches are clean and well-kept, and various activities are offered for both children and adults, including different types of watersports.

Another attraction in Jūrmala is the recently opened Līvu Akvapark – the largest water theme park in northern Europe. It covers an area of 39,600 square feet and has seven waterslides, wave pools and whirlpools, and its own river.

Jūrmala's main street is a one mile-long pedestrian zone. Here there are many souvenir shops where traditional Latvian crafts can be bought, including amber, crocheted hats, ceramics, and jewelry. On warm summer nights, bands perform in the cafés. At the end of the main street is the concert hall, which offers a varied program of events, including classical and pop concerts.

Aglona

Aglona lies between the towns of Krāslava and Preiļi in the province of Latgale. It represents the heart of Latvian Catholicism. According to legend, a young girl once saw a vision of the Virgin Mary here, and since then the town has been a site of pilgrimage. In the eighteenth century, Dominican monks built a monastery here, and later added the church of Aglona with two high bell towers. Over the main altar hangs a painting of Our Lady, which can only be seen on the night of August 15, when it is revealed for 10 minutes during mass. It is covered by another painting for the rest of the year. Thousands of pilgrims come to tiny Aglona from all over Latvia on this date, and many believe that the painting can cause miracles to happen. Pope John Paul II visited Aglona in 1993.

▼ *Every year, thousands of pilgrims make the trip to Aglona for the Feast of the Assumption of the Virgin Mary.*

People and culture

Latvia has a population of about 2.3 million. Nearly one third of the people live in the capital, Riga. A variety of languages can be heard in the city – 46 percent of the population are not Latvian by birth, and Latvian is the first language of only one third of the people.

▲ Handmade articles, such as gloves, hats and socks are sold in the street by St. Peter's Church in Riga.

▲ A Latvian woman dancing in the street to music from a tape recorder

Latvia has always been an international country. Before the Second World War, the population was 75 percent Latvian. The rest of the population consisted of Germans, Jews, Russians, Roma (Gypsies), Poles, and Lithuanians. In 1925, one in eight inhabitants was German, but later on all Germans in the Baltic countries were ordered to move to the areas of Poland that had become part of the German Empire. Only a few Germans live in Latvia now.

A small community is also all that remains of the Jewish population that made up 5 percent of the Latvian population before the Second World War. There are Jewish mass graves in the Bikernieku forest near Riga. The Jewish museum in the capital tells the history of the Jews in the city and explains what happened to them during the German occupation of World War II. Many Latvian Gypsies also died in this period.

In their turn, the communist occupiers conducted mass deportations between 1941 and 1949, exiling more than 200,000 inhabitants of Latvia to Siberia. Many of these people died, and only a few returned to Latvia. The Occupation Museum of Latvia tells the story of this tragedy.

◀ Livu Square in Riga in 1947

◀ *Most of the factories in Riga date from the period of Russian rule.*

After the Second World War, Latvia became part of the Soviet Union, and many new factories were constructed in Riga. Laborers from all over the Soviet Union arrived in Latvia to make up the workforce. This is one of the main reasons for all the different languages spoken in Latvia. In rural areas, however, Latvian remains the main language.

Language

The Latvian language is related to Lithuanian, and belongs to the Indo-European family of languages. It uses the Latin alphabet, but some vowels have diacritic marks, or accents, over them. Vowels that have a line over them are pronounced longer than ordinary vowels. The letters over or under which a comma is added are spoken more softly and a 'j' sound is added before the letter.

Many historians believe that Latvians had a written language before they were conquered by the Germans in the thirteenth century. After this, only oral history remained. Many Latvians today have gained most of their knowledge about the history of their land and people from folksongs and poetry that have been passed down from generation to generation. There are more than 1.5 million traditional folksongs in Latvia, reflecting the saying: "Every Latvian has his own folksongs." Latvians are fond of talking about their history. Folksongs and verses were ways of recording their history in difficult times when it was impossible to write it down.

▲ *On this sign, there is a horizontal line above the "a" and the "e," meaning that the letters are pronounced long.*

Animism

Although there are many churches in Latvia, and masses are held all over the country, with church bells ringing out, Latvia is not a particularly religious country. Many Latvians do not follow an organized religion. A god is celebrated in the old folksongs – a deity who dresses in a gray robe and walks through the fields blessing the harvest. This god was accompanied by Laima, the adviser of humanity and the one responsible for determining their fate. Laima does not belong in a church. She is a creature of nature, and can be found in many places, such as great oak trees, large stones lying in the middle of fields, or in the bark of a birch tree. This belief is called "animism."

Christian missionaries tried to convert the Latvians from their traditional animist faith for more than 800 years. However, many people continued to bring offerings of flowers to the same gods that their ancestors worshipped. When the first independent Republic of Latvia was declared in 1918, animism was strengthened by officials and proclaimed an official religion. Although animism is still an important part of ancient customs and beliefs, Christianity also plays a significant part in Latvian spiritual life today.

Christianity

The main religions in Latvia are Lutheranism, Roman Catholicism, and Russian Orthodox. In the Soviet era there was no freedom of religion, and many churches were closed or used for other purposes – the cathedral in Riga was used as a concert hall and museum, for example, and the Russian Orthodox Church was turned into a planetarium, an exhibition hall, and a café. Today, mass is held in these churches once more.

The largest group of Russian Orthodox Latvians lives in the Latgale area. One of the most famous churches is the Grebenscikova church, close to the center of Riga. This wooden church dates from 1814, and has golden domes and a façade that is covered with icons. The people who go there belong to a sect of the Russian Orthodox Church called the Old Believers. Women must cover their heads before they enter the church, and men without beards are forbidden.

▲ *A Russian Orthodox church in Rezekne, in eastern Latvia*

▶ *Most festivals are celebrated with a feast, shared with friends and family.*

Celebrations and festivals

Many festivals and holidays are celebrated in Latvia. This is because the majority of the population is of Russian descent, and still uses the "Julian" calendar. This is different from the calendar used in the west – the "Gregorian" calendar. Latvians celebrate Christmas, New Year's Eve and Easter twice – once for each calendar. Many Latvians celebrate the traditional Christian holidays once with family, and the second time with friends or colleagues, who might use another calendar.

The ancient Latvians followed the course of the sun through the sky, and celebrated the solstices when one season ended and the next began. The summer solstice is still celebrated with Līgo night and Jāņi day. The celebration of the winter solstice has been strongly influenced by Christian traditions. In ancient times, the people of the Baltic region celebrated the moment that the sun moved towards spring to herald the end of a long, dark winter. After Christianity came to the area, this festival was combined with Christmas traditions. There are still elements of the pagan rituals in the celebrations at this time of year. In rural areas, people walk through the streets in procession, pulling sleighs and wearing masks. They dress up as bears in furs, bearded Gypsies, or Death carrying his scythe.

The summer solstice, or Midsummer Eve, is also celebrated as a pagan festival. This is the name day of Jānis, a god worshipped by the ancient Latvians, who would come to Earth on Midsummer's Day and bring luck and fertility to the people.

In the old days, people cleaned their houses and made wreaths of oak leaves on Midsummer's Day. At night, they would eat cheese, drink beer, and sing songs. Many Latvians still celebrate in this way. A fire is lit, and part of the festivities includes jumping over this. Legends say that the flower of the fern will blossom on that night and that whoever finds the flower in the forest will be able to understand the languages of the birds and animals, and will find hidden treasures. In fact, the fern is not a flowering plant, but this is still part of the ancient Latvian folk tales.

◀ *Women dress in traditional Latvian costumes for celebrations such as Midsummer's Eve.*

In addition to their own and Christian holidays such as Christmas and Easter, Latvians celebrate other festivals that have been adopted from different countries, including Halloween and Valentine's Day. Many cultural events also end with large celebrations. A song festival has taken place in Latvia once every four years for more than a century. During this festival, a choir of more than 10,000 people comes together to sing. The best choirs and folk dance groups come to the festival from all over Latvia.

Katarina was born in the Netherlands. Her father is Dutch and her mother is from Latvia. "I moved to Latvia ten years ago," she explains. "I wanted to see where my mother came from." Katarina did not plan on remaining in Latvia, but she loved the country and its people so much that she stayed for several years.

Now back in the Netherlands, she is the director of a Latvian business in Amsterdam. She celebrates the Midsummer festival with other Latvians who live in the Netherlands.

▲ Music and folksongs are an important part of any festival in Latvia.

Technology

Technology is developing quickly in Latvia. The number of people owning mobile phones increases daily. More and more people are also buying computers for use at home, and just about every school in Latvia has a computer room. Those without their own computers can use them at Internet cafés, which can be found in almost every city. Young people in particular find them very useful, and enjoy sending e-mail messages to their friends, and spending time in Internet chat rooms.

There are more than 60 radio stations in Latvia, although many of them only broadcast to local areas, and around 75 television stations. Foreign programs are also transmitted on Latvian television.

Government

Latvia is a parliamentary democracy, which means that the citizens vote to elect members to represent them in parliament. The Latvian constitution is called *satverse*, and was first established in 1922. It has been amended a few times since then, but Latvian politics are still based on this constitution.

The people elect the parliament – the Saeima – every four years. During the elections, citizens vote for the candidate of the party they want to see in government. There are more than 20 political parties in Latvia, and candidates will gain a seat in parliament if they get more than five percent of the votes. Because of this, the government is made up of a coalition of many different parties. There are 100 members of parliament, who represent various political standpoints.

The president is the head of state, and is elected by the Saeima every three years. He or she is helped by a council of advisers. A proposal is currently being discussed in which the president would be elected directly by the people of Latvia. The prime minister is the head of the government and is chosen by the president.

▲ *Because the government is made up of representatives of several different parties, there are often heated debates in parliament.*

▼ *Mrs. Vaira Vike-Freiberga was elected president of Latvia in 1999.*

LATVIA

Education

In Latvia, children must attend school between the ages of 7 and 16. In 2002, a law was put into place which stated that children aged five and six must also go to pre-school. Young Latvians know that a good education is important, and many of them choose to continue their schooling even after the age of 16.

In Latvia, parents can choose whether to send their children to a private school or a state school from nursery age. However, private schools are expensive, and only the very wealthy can afford them.

Compulsory education in Latvia is divided into years 1 to 9. Year 1 starts at the age of seven in primary school. Up to year 4, children are given a general (basic) education and are taught by a single teacher. In years 5 to 9, specialist subject teachers cover a range of areas such as languages, math, and science.

In rural areas, classes can be as small as only eight children, but the law also says that there cannot be more than 34 pupils in one class. In smaller schools, there are sometimes mixed-age classes, but generally, children are taught with others of the same age. The curriculum is the same in all schools. Each year, all classes have a project week, where pupils have to write an essay or give a presentation about a subject of their choice. Many choose to tell others about the history of their town. They take this very seriously, and visit libraries and museums, as well as interviewing people from the neighborhood.

◀ In city schools, like this one in Riga, classes are limited to 34 pupils. Children of this age are taught subjects such as math, music, and art by one teacher.

▶ *A secondary school in Daugavpils*

Some subjects are compulsory from year 1. These include the Latvian language, math, physical education, music, and art. In year 5, pupils start to learn history and home economics. Geography and biology begin in year 6, but the other sciences – chemistry and physics – are not taught until year 8.

School children in Latvia have four main holidays a year. These are usually one week in the autumn, two weeks at Christmas, one week for a break in the spring, and nearly three months for summer vacation.

Secondary education

Once pupils have completed their period of compulsory education, they can go on to secondary schools. These are intended to help teenagers prepare for higher education or for particular jobs. There are general secondary schools and vocational secondary schools. At vocational schools, students can train for a whole range of different jobs, including car mechanics, nursing, photography, computer programming, and secretarial work. General secondary schools continue more academic training. There are also professional technical secondary schools, which provide the opportunity to combine a general secondary education with professional training. Almost every city has a music school and an art school. Because many young people from Latvia want to attend these schools, they often have halls of residence for the students to live in.

▼ *A school in Cesis, in central Latvia*

▼ *Teenagers spend their spare time with friends.*

Jūlija is in year 7. "I live in Riga," she explains. "I go to school every day except Sunday. I learn how to play the piano at music school. I have to leave home early in the morning, because the school is in the center of the city and I live quite a long way away. It takes half an hour by bus from my home to the school, and it's usually packed at that time of day. Lessons usually last until the afternoon, but sometimes we have to stay longer to finish an assignment. Last Christmas, we rehearsed a short play, *Snow White and the Seven Dwarves*. I was the fourth dwarf. We learn a lot at school. I like music and drawing, but I don't like math. I have piano lessons twice a week, on Tuesdays and Thursdays, in addition to my lessons at music school. On Saturdays, I go to music school, but on Sundays, I watch television or play on the computer. Sometimes I go out and meet up with my friends who live nearby. We go into Riga and look at the shops or get ice cream or a drink and just hang out together."

Higher education

There are several universities and colleges of higher education in Latvia, many of which specialize in particular subjects. The most famous is the University of Latvia in Riga, but educational facilities such as universities and polytechnics have been established in other areas, too. Professions that are related to the arts can only be taught in Riga, because the music academy, the art academy, and the cultural academy are all located there.

Higher education, such as undergraduate programs, usually lasts for four years in Latvia, and must be paid for by the student, although some special grants are made to students who are very gifted. The number of scholarships available is very low, however, and students often have to rely on their parents to help pay for their education. If this isn't possible, they may have to get a job while continuing their studies. Students can also apply for loans for education at a state polytechnic, which they can pay back at a later time.

▶ *Students in the library at the University of Latvia in Riga*

Cuisine

There are many delicious traditional dishes from Latvia, and these are served at restaurants and cafés across the country. Latvians use lots of fresh produce in their recipes, including mushrooms and berries, which many people go to the forests and gather themselves to make into sauces and jams.

Traditional food

In the morning, the cafés in the cities smell of coffee and apple cake cooked with cinnamon. Many people eat cereal for breakfast – muesli or cornflakes, with milk or yogurt. Biezpiens (cottage cheese) with sour cream and chives is also very popular, and is often eaten with sweet-bread rolls.

For lunch, cafés and restaurants serve many different kinds of salads, with vegetables, cheese, and meat. Bread accompanies most meals, and rye bread is especially good in Latvia, made with cumin, malt syrup, and honey.

▼ *Many people in Latvia prefer to buy their food at the markets, where produce is fresh and healthier.*

▶ *Many kinds of cheese, yogurt and other dairy products are sold in the markets.*

▼ *Cafés and restaurants serve a variety of healthy salads and fresh dishes for lunch.*

Potatoes are a typical ingredient of traditional Latvian dishes. They are prepared in many different ways, but one of the most popular is to bake them in the oven with the skin still on. Often they are baked with marinated herrings. Latvians then eat them served with cottage cheese. On Sundays, people often make potato cakes. Another traditional Latvian dish is marrowfat peas served with bacon.

Latvians also like to try out new recipes, and cookbooks are very popular in the country. There are many television programs about cooking, including some in which famous people prepare their favorite dishes. Usually, these are exotic dishes that they have tried during a trip abroad. Latvians are great fans of international cuisine, and many restaurants serve foreign food, such as Mexican, sushi, or Greek.

Recipe for potato cakes

Ingredients
2 lbs. potatoes
3 eggs
Salt
Flour

Grate the potatoes and dry them on kitchen paper. Beat the eggs and add them to the potatoes, with a pinch of salt and some flour. Add some flavor with ground pepper, curry, or stock powder. Put one spoon of batter after another into a pan, and fry the cakes in the oil until they are golden brown on both sides. Traditionally, these cakes are served with sour blueberry jam or with sour cream.

◀ *Children learn how to hunt for and pick mushrooms and berries at a young age.*

Fresh produce

All kinds of food can be bought in shops and markets – food produced in Latvia as well as imported goods such as bananas and melons. However, many Latvians go to the forest with baskets in summer and autumn to pick berries and look for mushrooms themselves. Strawberries can be picked at the end of June and in July. After this, other berries are in season. Wild raspberries grow in the clearings, and blackberries can be found deeper in the woodlands. Cranberries grow in swampy areas, and there are also bitter rowan berries, which are used to make wine, or mixed with apples to make a jam.

In the late summer and early autumn, all kinds of fruits, jams and preserves are available in the markets, and people even set up stalls on street corners to sell their home-made produce.

Mushroom-picking is also a popular pastime in Latvia. Friends and families organize competitions for finding the most mushrooms in the forests. Many different types of mushrooms grow there, including chanterelles, boletuses, and ceps. The mushrooms are often fried and served with a creamy sauce, and accompanied with potatoes. They can also be marinated or dried, then stored in jars to be eaten throughout the winter when fresh mushrooms are not available.

▲ *Different types of mushrooms can be found in the Latvian woodlands.*

◀ *People buy home-made preserves at the market.*

▲ ▶ *Huge indoor markets sell just about everything people need in the way of fresh food, including meat, cheese, fruit, and vegetables.*

Farm produce

Under the communist regime, all farms were forced to produce the same crops. Every farm grew potatoes and raised cows, pigs and chickens. Nowadays, farms still have these things, but many have begun to branch out and specialize in particular crops or livestock. Some farms have goats, and goats' cheese is becoming increasingly popular. On other farms, small, colorful birds called lapwings are bred, and their eggs are now sold in many places.

Ostriches thrive in the Latvian climate and there are even farms that raise these birds. People have to book in advance to enjoy an omelette made of ostrich eggs. Many restaurants in Riga have contracts with the ostrich farms, and have "local" ostrich steaks on the menu.

Herbs are common in Latvian cuisine, especially dill and chives. Some farmers grow these and many other types of herb, such as oregano, thyme, and coriander.

Honey

Latvia has a long tradition of beekeeping. Honey and beeswax are often mentioned in folk tales and symbolize prosperity. Latvian honey can be light yellow or dark brown, depending on the type of flower from which the bees gathered the nectar. There are many different flavors, but the honey is always sweet. Dieticians often advise using honey instead of sugar in recipes and drinks, because it is much better for you. Hot lime-blossom tea with honey is a traditional cure for a cold.

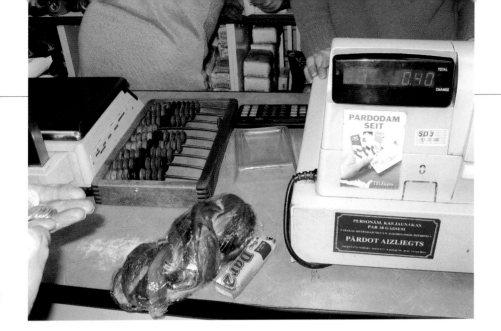

◀ ▼ *Fresh bread is available in even the small corner shops in the villages, as is the Latvian specialty chocolate from the Laima company.*

Desserts

Another Latvian specialty is chocolate. Laima chocolate, made in Latvia, is known in many countries. The Laima factory has been running for more than 100 years, and is still making new types of chocolate. There are Laima shops all over Latvia.

Other sweet dishes popular in Latvia include kringel, a coffee cake that is traditionally made as a birthday cake, and apple loaf, served with sugar and cinnamon. Various fruit sauces are made with all the fresh berries people collect, and these are delicious served over ice cream or baked desserts.

Drink

Beer is a popular drink among Latvians, and there are several breweries across the country. The most famous is the Aldaris brewery in Riga, and the beer made here is exported to many European countries. There is also a traditional Latvian alcoholic drink called Riga Black Balsam, which has been produced in the country since 1755 – but it doesn't taste very nice!

▶ *Different types of bottled beer produced at the Aldaris brewery in Riga. The brewery was established in 1865, and as well as beer, it also produces mineral water and soft drinks.*

Transportation

Latvia is a major trade route between the countries of Western Europe, Northern Europe, and Russia. Every day hundreds of cargo trucks travel through the country, carrying products such as gasoline, timber, food, and textiles. However, for locals and visitors to get around, various means of public transportation are provided, which are usually efficient and cheap.

▼ *Country roads are often riddled with potholes. These areas can cause problems for drivers, especially in the winter.*

There are around 37,000 miles of roads in Latvia. The highways are usually well-surfaced and traveling on the main roads is easy and efficient, as these are the main transport routes through the country, running from one end to the other. However, to explore Latvia thoroughly, it is best to take the minor roads through the countryside, although these are not always so well-maintained.

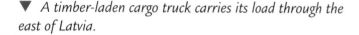

▼ *A timber-laden cargo truck carries its load through the east of Latvia.*

These girls are waiting for a bus at the busy bus station in Daugavpils. They live in a nearby village and attend school in the city. "We like coming into Daugavpils," they explain. "It's a big city and is always very lively. It's easy to get to because public transport is good – buses in particular run frequently between the cities and villages like ours. They're also useful for getting round within the towns if you don't want to walk around."

Buses

Buses are the most popular means of transportation in Latvia. From the central terminal in Riga they travel to most parts of Latvia, as well as to several other European cities. Visitors who want to travel around within the capital often take the trolleybus – a kind of bus that is powered by overhead electric wires. There are also trams in Riga, which are slower than the trolleybuses, but offer a more leisurely view of the city. Minibuses are another popular means of transportation around the cities, and these are the fastest way to get from place to place. However, at busy times, there can often be long lines for the minibuses. They usually run every five to ten minutes.

Traffic can be very heavy in the cities, particularly Riga. Traffic in and out of the capital has to travel over one of the three bridges over the Daugava River – the stone bridge, the suspension bridge, or the island bridge – and this can cause delays, especially during rush hour.

▶ Buses are the quickest and most convenient way of traveling around the larger cities in Latvia.

▼ Traffic can be bumper-to-bumper across the Daugava bridges in Riga.

◄ *The station in Riga contains a shopping center and cafés.*

Cycling

Bicycles are a popular and fun way of traveling around towns and villages in Latvia. They are becoming more common in the larger cities as well. It is often quicker to cycle somewhere in Riga than to use public transportation, as it avoids getting stuck in traffic jams.

Railways

There are around 1,550 miles of railway lines across Latvia. The train is a fast and convenient means of traveling between destinations. The Central Station in Riga is always very busy, but this is because it houses a large shopping center, and many cafés and restaurants. Locals do their shopping there after work or meet friends in the cafés. From the station, though, it is possible to catch trains to the beach, which takes less than an hour, or to many other towns and villages across the country.

▼ *A train runs twice a day on the narrow track between the towns of Alüksne and Gulbene. The tracks were laid in 1910.*

► *Liepāja Harbor*

Shipping

One of the most pleasant ways of getting around and enjoying Riga is by traveling on the Daugava by boat. This is especially popular in the summer season, when tourists can sit on the deck, enjoying a glass of wine in the sunshine. Areas such as Mežaparka and Jūrmala can also be reached by boat. The *Hercogs Jekabs* travels down the Venta River from Ventspils.

The ports of Latvia are used predominately by freighters and some passenger ships. There are ferries between Riga and the Swedish capital Stockholm, and between Riga and various parts of Germany. Another ferry connects Ventspils to Sweden and Germany. Cruise ships also call in at Riga, offering their passengers a few hours to explore Latvia's capital.

Aviation

There are three main airports in Latvia – in Riga, Liepaja, and Ventspils. All of them offer flights to international destinations. The airport at Riga has recently been renovated. On the top level are the offices belonging to the various airline companies. Latvia's national airline is AirBaltic.

◄ *Riga International Airport is the largest airport in the Baltic states. In 2004 it served over one million passengers.*

The economy

For many years the Latvian economy was run by the state under Soviet rule. However, in recent years the country has moved towards a market economy and has made many changes. These include removing price controls and privatizing many businesses. Farmers in particular have benefited, as they are now allowed to own their land and decide what crops to raise.

Latvia lies at the junction of several trade routes. In the past, this has made it attractive to invading peoples, who have levied taxes on other countries who wanted to travel through Latvian territory. Although Latvia is still a main trade route between European countries, today the Latvian economy is competitive. It exports several products to countries around the world, and the quality of Latvian produce is high.

Import and export

Timber is one of Latvia's most important natural resources, and wood and wood products are the country's main export. However, there have recently been concerns that the rate of deforestation in Latvia is too high, and the effect on the environment could be damaging. Other exports include machinery and textiles. Underwear from the Lauma Company is exported to many countries, as are cosmetics from the Dzintars factory.

Foodstuffs are another major export product. Canned foods from Latvia are in high demand in countries like Russia, in particular the traditional Latvian Baltic herring in oil (also called sprot). Latvian honey and beeswax are major exports, and beekeepers pride themselves on the quality of their goods, which have a good reputation in the international market. Ointments made from these products are also an important industry. Other export products are the medicines produced by the high-tech factory Olainfarm – the largest pharmaceutical manufacturer in the Baltic states.

The main imports in Latvia are machinery and heavy equipment, chemicals, fuel, and vehicles, but more everyday products from many other countries can also be found in the supermarkets and shops. These are mainly foodstuffs that are not available in Latvia, such as soy sauce from Korea and popular Mexican foods.

◀ *Although the export of timber is important to the Latvian economy, people are growing concerned that this resource will be depleted too quickly.*

◀ Basic foodstuffs like potatoes are key to Latvia's economy.

Although plenty of fruit grows in Latvia, the country imports other types, such as pineapples and lychees. Despite this, people are encouraged to buy Latvian products to help the economy, and Latvians are happy to do so, usually purchasing home-grown products such as apples and cheese.

Amber

Amber is created deep underwater, where the sap of trees from millions of years ago became hard as stone. The historian Plinius recorded that Emperor Nero sent his servants to travel to the coast of the Baltic countries on horseback to search for amber with which to decorate the Roman circus. Amber has been an important Latvian export product for centuries. Today, tourists still buy amber bracelets and other items of jewelry carefully crafted in Latvia. With luck, it is even possible to find small pieces of amber on the beaches, especially after a storm. Amber is also called "sunstone."

Currency

Latvia's national currency is the lat (LVL), and the coins are called santimes. The Latvians have an emotional connection to their currency, which was introduced shortly after Latvian independence. During the Soviet occupation, rubles and kopeks were used, just like in other areas of the Soviet Union. Many women, however, wore brooches made of silver lat coins. One face of these coins showed the coat of arms of independent Latvia, and the other side showed the profile of a girl. This girl with braids in her hair, wearing Latvian national dress and a wreath with pearls around her head, became the symbol of an independent Latvia. After regaining independence in 1992, the lat was reintroduced. There are coins of 1, 2, 5, 10, 20 and 50 santimes and of 1 and 2 lats, and banknotes of 5, 10, 20, 50, 100 and 500 lats.

The 1-lat coin shows a salmon, which can be found in the Baltic Sea. The 2-lat coin depicts a cow. On the 5-lat banknote, the birch tree – a symbol of strength and endurance – is shown. Every year, the national bank of Latvia introduces a new coin, and these have won several awards in international competitions.

One lat equals about $1.75.

◄ Farmers work all year round to raise produce to sell within Latvia and to export to other countries.

Agriculture

The main agricultural products in Latvia are grain, sugar beets, potatoes, vegetables, and a variety of dairy products. However, cultivating grain can be difficult – too many days without rain and the crops will dry out; too much rain and the crops may not grow. Rye, wheat, corn, and oats are also grown in Latvia. Immediately after the harvest, the grain is ground into flour and bakers begin to make all different types of bread. Many traditional recipes for bread have been preserved, and at bakeries you can buy wholemeal bread with cranberries, bread with nuts or honey, and bread with carrots. There is also sweet-and-sour bread, made with half ordinary flour and half rye.

The city of Sabile in Courland (Kurzeme) is mentioned in the *Guinness Book of Records*. The highest northern vineyards in the world are found here. Wine has been produced in Sabile since the sixteenth century. It used to be well known in other countries, but wine export decreased in the twentieth century. Today, the wine growers from Sabile hope to regain their former reputation.

Energy

Latvia does not have a mining industry or oil, which is why it has to import gasoline and raw materials for the factories. Forty-seven percent of all energy requirements are imported.

▼ A famer plows his fields to prepare them for next year's crops.

▲ Wine-making has been an important industry in Latvia for centuries.

Nature

Latvia has two important nature reserves, the Kemeru National Park and the Gauja National Park. The Gauja National Park is older, and is located in Vidzeme, on the banks of the Gauja River. The park is 62 miles long and 25 miles wide.

▼ *The Gauja National Park is a popular tourist attraction because of the diversity of wildlife and plants that are found there.*

Three towns lie within the Gauja National Park: Sigulda, Legatne, and Cesis. This area has been carefully preserved and there are many natural features within its boundaries. High rocks of yellow-brown sandstone and caves can be found all along the banks of the Gauja. The most famous of the caves is the Gutmana Cave in Sigulda, which is 30 feet high and 46 feet deep. Lovers have come here for centuries and left their inscriptions carved into the cave walls. According to legend, a tragic love story between a girl, Maija, also called "Turaidas Roze" (Rose of Turaida) and Viktor, a gardener of the castle, was played out here. There are several ruins of medieval castles in the area. The renovated Castle of Turaidas now holds a museum. There are many walking and cycle routes marked in the Gauja National Park for tourists, and it is also possible to travel down the Gauja River by boat.

Animals

Latvia is home to many species of animals. Rabbits, deer, fox, and elk all thrive here, especially in the large forested areas. There are plenty of otters, too. However, there are a few rare species of animal that are on the verge of extinction, including martens and ermine. Some forests contain wolves and brown bears, which occasionally wander into Latvia from Russia or Estonia.

The brown bear, which may be seen in some animal parks, is the most dangerous of all the animals found in Latvia. There are also large deer roaming these areas. However, because these parks are designed to maintain the animals' natural environment, they can be difficult to spot, as most are very shy. Wild horses have long been extinct in Latvia, but a few have recently been brought to an island in Pope Lake, where they now live. Wild cattle have been added to the animal population of the island as well.

One animal mentioned in many Latvian folksongs is the grass snake. Farmers leave a saucer of milk on the doorstep for grass snakes to come from the nearby forest to drink. There is only one poisonous snake in Latvia – the viper, which can often be seen in the trees, basking in the sunshine. Vipers are usually not dangerous as long as they are left alone.

▲ Oak leaves (top) and leaves of the lime tree (bottom) – two of the most common trees found in Latvia.

Many birds come to Riga and other Latvian cities to live for the winter. Some of them are species that usually migrate to much warmer areas. Brightly colored mandarin ducks were spotted near the Riga Channel a few years ago, and people wondered whether they had escaped from the zoo!

In spring, the migratory birds that leave Latvia each winter return. Owls and doves are common in Latvia. In rural areas, storks make their nests in telephone poles and pylons. Many farms put up masts especially to invite storks to nest there, because Latvians think that storks are lucky (see page 15).

Brother oak, sister lime tree

The oak and the lime tree are often mentioned in Latvian folksongs. The old Latvian warriors made their shields from tough oak wood. Men wear a crown of oak leaves during the Midsummer Night festival. The oak symbolizes power and trust. Farmers used to plant oak trees on fallow land because they thought they were attractive and that they provided a homey feel. Large oak trees are now characteristic of the Latvian landscape.

In Latvian folksongs, the lime tree is the symbol of femininity. In these songs, a lime tree standing next to an oak tree symbolizes a strong and stable family. Latvians believe that lime-blossom tea is the best cure for a cold. Dried lime blossoms can be bought at the drugstore, but the tea is supposed to taste best when it is made from the petals of hand-picked, fresh flowers. Instead of sugar, Latvians add a spoonful of lime-blossom honey to their tea. Many Latvian families drink this tea in the evening.

Plants and flowers

Latvia is a country of forests and meadows. According to tradition, houses must be decorated with flowers and birch twigs during midsummer Jāņi festivities. People adorn themselves with flowers, too. Every person has a different garland. It is not important whether it is very dramatic or elaborate, but the number of different herbs and flowers is significant. Three times nine (27) is thought to be a lucky number, and many people therefore weave 27 different plants into their garland. These are picked by hand from the meadows or forests. There are hundreds of types of flowers in Latvia, although most meadow flowers are small and inconspicuous. Wild orchids – pale cream or purple in color – grow in the forests, as do fragrant violets, but they should not be picked, as they are included in the Latvian Red Book – a list of endangered flora and fauna in the country.

Environmental issues

There are still many environmental issues to be addressed in Latvia. One of the biggest problems is deforestation. Timber is the primary export product, and it brings in a lot of money. Unfortunately, large parts of the old forests are being cut down, and not enough new trees are being planted. Unless solutions are found, this could eventually become a huge problem.

Illegal dumping of garbage is another problem. There are many organizations for environmental protection that fight this. One of these organizations is Pedas (which means "Tracks"), and many well-known Latvians are members of this group – musicians, athletes, and artists. They regularly organize clean-up days, and try to attract as many people as possible to attend them. At these events people remove trash from the forests and meadows, and take it to garbage dumps. Nowadays, many schools organize similar activities to keep their environment clean.

Another serious environmental problem that has arisen in the last few years is the construction of an oil terminal at Butinge in Lithuania. The environmental organization VAK strongly protested against this. In spite of all the protests, the oil terminal was built. It has resulted in a number of incidents of oil pollution off the Latvian coast.

The organization Green Point is also very active in Latvia. Its goal is to convince people to separate the contents of their trash. Unfortunately, most trash is still thrown out together, without being separated for recycling purposes.

Latvian waters are rich in fish. Unfortunately, many people abuse this fact by fishing illegally. Environmentalists are worried that fish stocks may soon be depleted. In recent years, strategies have been established to save the salmon, and many illegal fisheries have been closed down.

▲ *This young girl is helping collect garbage as part of a campaign organized by the environmental group Pedas.*

Raima became a member of the Environmental Protection Club when she was 14. "I was not allowed to join earlier," she explains. "Before then, however, I helped out at the club because my parents were members. They believe strongly that we should fight for our environment, and that it is not only the large factories that pollute it. People just don't realize what they are doing when they throw plastic bags away in the streets. They will remain there until they are excavated in hundreds of years. The people then will think we were a society of plastic-bag worshippers! My friends and I distribute notes that explain how wrong some of our actions are. I hope that at least some of the people understand."

Latvia in Europe

Latvia became a full member of the European
Union on May 1, 2004. This was a significant step
for the country in terms of developing important
relationships with other European countries,
as well as those in the wider world.

Latvia enjoys a good relationship with the two other Baltic countries – Estonia and Lithuania.
These three states have a lot in common. They all became independent on the same day after the
First World War, and they experienced their economic booms at the same time. The three countries
were simultaneously occupied by Soviet forces after the Second World War, and became independent
again at the same time. Despite this, Latvia, Estonia, and Lithuania are very different in many respects,
each with their own language, national dress, and traditions.

Latvia also has good relationships with other northern European countries such as Finland, Sweden,
and Denmark. Some of these countries are within easy reach of Latvia – it is only a few hours from Riga
to Stockholm in Sweden by ferry. Many Latvians emigrated to Sweden during the Second World War,
and never returned to Latvia, so there are large communities of Latvians living there. Many Latvians also
live in Germany, and for a long time there was a Latvian school in Munster. However, today most
children of Latvian immigrants who want to learn the language of their homeland can actually study
in Latvia itself. After the Second World War, during the period of Soviet rule, Latvians living in other
countries tried to bring the plight of their country to international attention. It was this campaigning
that eventually helped lead to all three of the Baltic countries gaining independence.

There are many ties of friendship and treaties of cooperation between Latvian cities and those in other
countries. The cities with which Riga shares these ties are are Bremen (Germany), Kobe (Japan), Venice
(Italy), and Amsterdam (The Netherlands).

▶ In May of 1990, crowds
celebrate the news that
Latvia will no longer be part
of the Soviet Union, but an
independent republic.

International organizations

In a referendum, the people of Latvia voted in favor of their country joining the European Union. For older Latvians, this meant that the country would return to the Europe from which it had been separated by force at the beginning of the Second World War. They remember this as a Europe in which Latvian students attended famous universities and academies, in which Latvian artists could receive state aid in order to travel to countries such as France and Italy. They remember this as a period of development and prosperity, and hope that it will be so again.

As well as the European Union, Latvia is a member of several other international organizations, all of which will help it play an increasingly important role on the world stage. It was accepted as a member of NATO in 2004. It is also a member of the World Trade Organization, the World Health Organization, the Organization for Security and Co-operation in Europe and the United Nations Educational, Scientific and Cultural Organization (UNESCO).

▲ *A young Latvian girl in traditional costume stands by the flag of the European Union during the festivities to celebrate Latvia becoming a member of the organization.*

◀ *U.S. president George W. Bush with Latvian prime minister Indulis Emsis in Washington, D.C., during the inauguration in March 2004 of seven new countries into NATO.*

Iceland

Euro

N O R T H   S E A

Republic
of
Ireland

United Kingdom

The Net

Belgium

Luxemb

France

Switzerla

A T L A N T I C   O C E A N

Monaco

Portugal

Spain

M E D I T E R R A N E A

0   500 km

0   500 miles

Sweden

Finland

Norway

BALTIC SEA

Estonia

Latvia

Lithuania

Russian
Federation

Denmark

erlands

Germany

Poland

Belarus

urg

Czech
Republic

Slovakia

Ukraine

CASPIAN SEA

Austria

Hungary

Moldova

Slovenia

Romania

Croatia Bosnia
Herzegovina

ADRIATIC SEA

Yugoslavia

Bulgaria

BLACK SEA

Italy

Macedonia

Albania

Turkey

Greece

Malta

SEA

Cyprus